DEXTER'S DRAWINGS:

Are They Art?

Lawrence Abrams, author

Dexter Jacoby, illustrator

No Harm Press
New York NY

Copyright 2023 Lawrence Abrams

"All rights reserved ". No part of this book may be reproduced or transmitted in any form whatsoever without the author's prior written consent, except in the case of quotations embodied in critical articles or reviews. Permission requests may be addressed to querynoharmpress@gmail.com.

ISBN (eBook): 978-1-915642-39-4
ISBN (Paperback): 978-1-915642-36-3
ISBN (Hardcover): 978-1-915642-40-0

Library of Congress Control Number: 2024903198

Dedication

This picture book is dedicated to Dexter Jacoby who radiates joy into all that he touches as he grows into adulthood. The pictures represent his vision of things at age eleven. As a child grows his perspective will undoubtedly change and these images are a reminder of the innocence we all should cherish.

A Message from the Author

For years I have attempted to create a children's picture book for Dexter, my grandson, the way I had for his older sister Charlie. I failed consistently not able to find a story which suited his personality. One day Dexter shared his artwork with me and the more I studied it, the more I thought here is a springboard into an issue I wanted people to understand.

When people read the book they are asked to evaluate Dexter's art by tallying their responses on the enclosed spreadsheet.

The final section "Examine Critical Judgements" gives the reader a chance to reflect on the human values too often drowned out by the noise of living in an alienated society. Bullying, supported by intolerance, mockery of others, caste projections and the absence of deep personal connections due to ever increasing screen time contribute to a cruelty in our culture. We must responsibly address these problems in order to discover the wonder of what our children can become. This book is my small offering to that end.

About the Author and Illustrator

LAWRENCE ABRAMS is a retired high school principal in New York City, where he worked for several decades to reform public education and became an advocate for the small school movement. He is the author of two books. <u>The Grievance: On a Real Life-and-Death Story</u> and <u>Twenty Life Lessons</u>. In addition he authored a children's picture book, <u>Animal Tales</u>.

DEXTER JACOBY lives in Brooklyn, with his mother Meredith, older sister Charlie, and his father, Drew. In addition Stew Smith, his stepfather, and his sons, Atlas and Pilot are integral in Dexter's life. He loves drawing, coding, Roblox, and paddle boarding in the Berkshires.

Contents

1. Dexter's Self-Portrait 8
2. Multiple Eyes 10
3. Two Hands 12
4. Snail on a Stool 14
5. Pyramid Giving Birth 16
6. World Buildings 18
7. Half Face of Boy with a Dog 20
8. Two Bananas and an Apple 22
9. Still Life of a Soda Can 24
10. Elephant 26
11. Flying Dragon 28
12. Gray Smiling Fog 30
13. Fireworks 32
14. Sun Fireworks with Aurora 34
15. Rating Dexter's Drawings 36
16. Understand the Tally 37
17. Examine Critical Judgements 37
18. Dexter's Drawings: A Guided Discussion 38

The Challenge

Dexter challenges you to decide
If his drawings should not be denied

Is it merely boyish scribble
Or true art without a quibble?

In this picture book
On many a page
Are Dexter's drawings
In which you engage

Designed in art class
Taken after school
To play with your mind
And the golden rule

Is it art or fart?
Critics through ages
Debate the issue
To become sages

Dexter draws images
To express his vision
Do they soar like eagles
Or waddle like pigeons?

Art is ephemeral
It beckons viewers in
And speaks to lost souls
To devour their sin

Tactically farts lie there
With gases that repel
Inhale the aroma
You'd think you'd been in hell

Critics judge art after
Examining the work
Declaring the artist
Important or a jerk

Be bold and judge
With eyes that care
See the message
If one is there

Will you declare each work
An abomination?
Might it take the viewer
To a higher station?

A critic can be nasty or kind
Delving into the artist's mind.

Surgically look at the art
Then tally up if you are smart

You are invited to become an art critic by going to page 36. Follow the directions on the spreadsheet as you rate each drawing.

1. Dexter's Self-Portrait

Dexter's self-portrait
An image of a boy
Looking at the world
To discover joy

Imagine for a moment
He is staring into you
Wondering if your take
Of his artwork is true

2. Multiple Eyes

Many eyes see the way
Into your interior
Then wincing from gasses
In your posterior

The images eyes see
Projected to your brain
Maybe sharp or fuzzy
Or totally insane

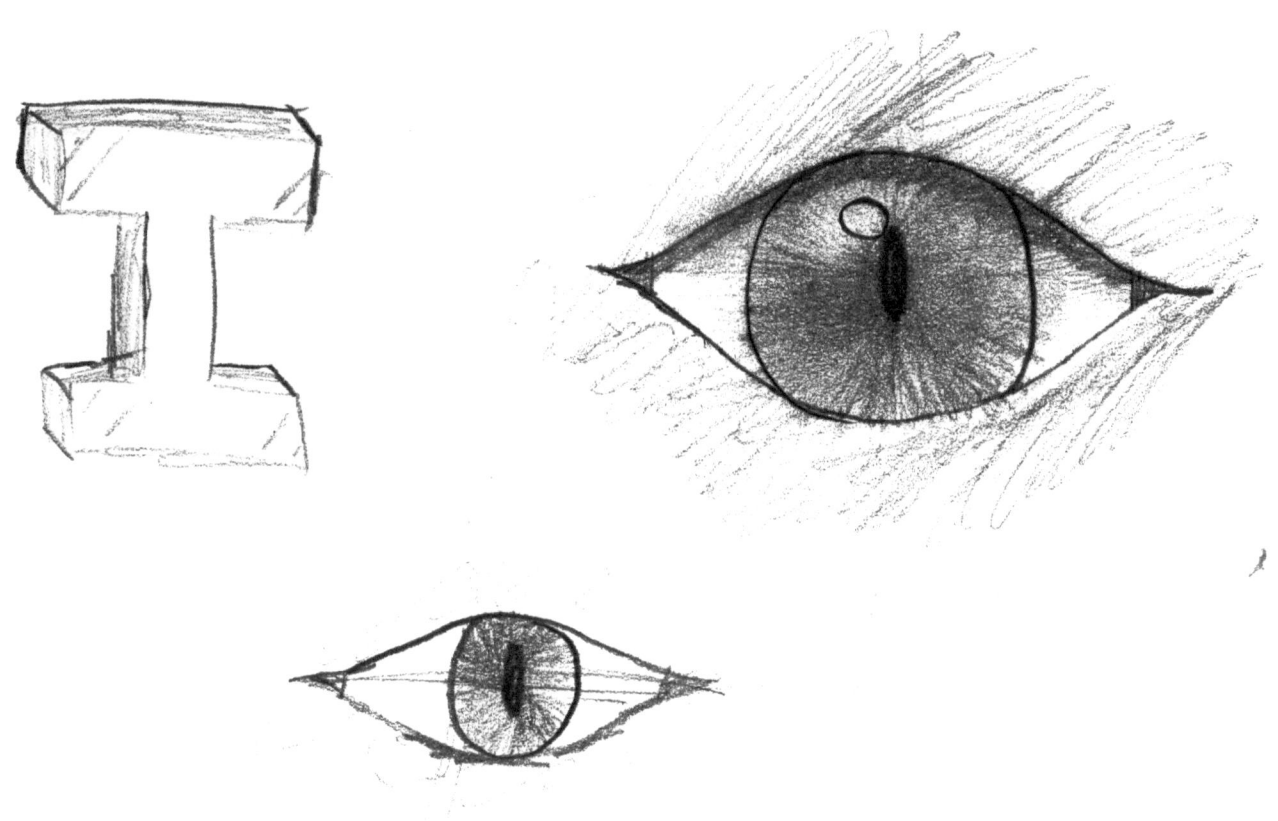

3. Two Hands

Fingers flexible
To draw the sublime
Creating an image
To stop points in time

With fingers so nimble
And a mind that is free
The artist can create
What the world should be

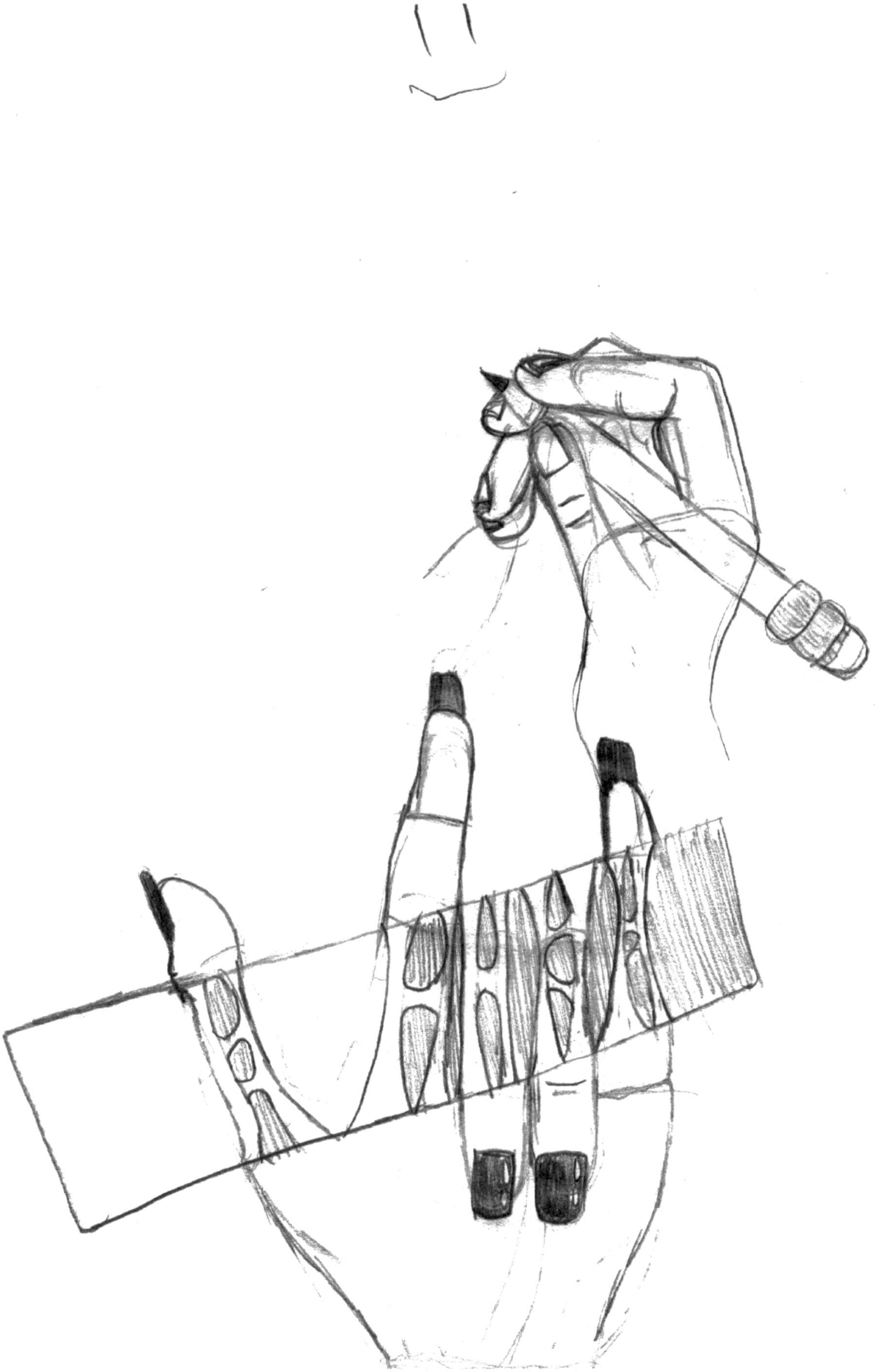

4. Snail on a Stool

Did you ever ponder why
A snail would sit on a stool?
To make the viewer happy
Happy cannot be cruel

What did bring you here
To this place so high?
To seek a better view
Or simply to defy?

5. Pyramid Giving Birth

**Witness the miracle of
A pyramid giving birth
Dropping baby structures
Softly landing on earth**

6. World Buildings

**The structures multiply
Reaching into the sky**

**Creating world cities
Not understanding why**

7. Half Face of Boy with a Dog

A boy and his dog
Within a city lies
Loving their friendship
Valuing their ties

The boy is eleven
The dog is old and brown
They are together
Their footing is sound

8. Two Bananas and an Apple

Is the banana's shadow
Something one must grapple?
Misty shadings of gray and
A solitary apple

Life has lurking shadows
Pensive and elusive
In the dim horizon
They are inconclusive

9. Still Life of a Soda Can

A simple can of soda pop
Smiling for good measure
Knowing its life's mission:
Giving sips of pleasure

The soda oh so sweet
Delicious in flavors
Invigorating souls
Of what one's life savours

10. Elephant

See the mighty elephant
With an elongated trunk
Protecting his family
From hunters who are drunk

The mightiest of creatures
Can be felled by those who drink
Weapons of mass destruction
Populate our world with stink

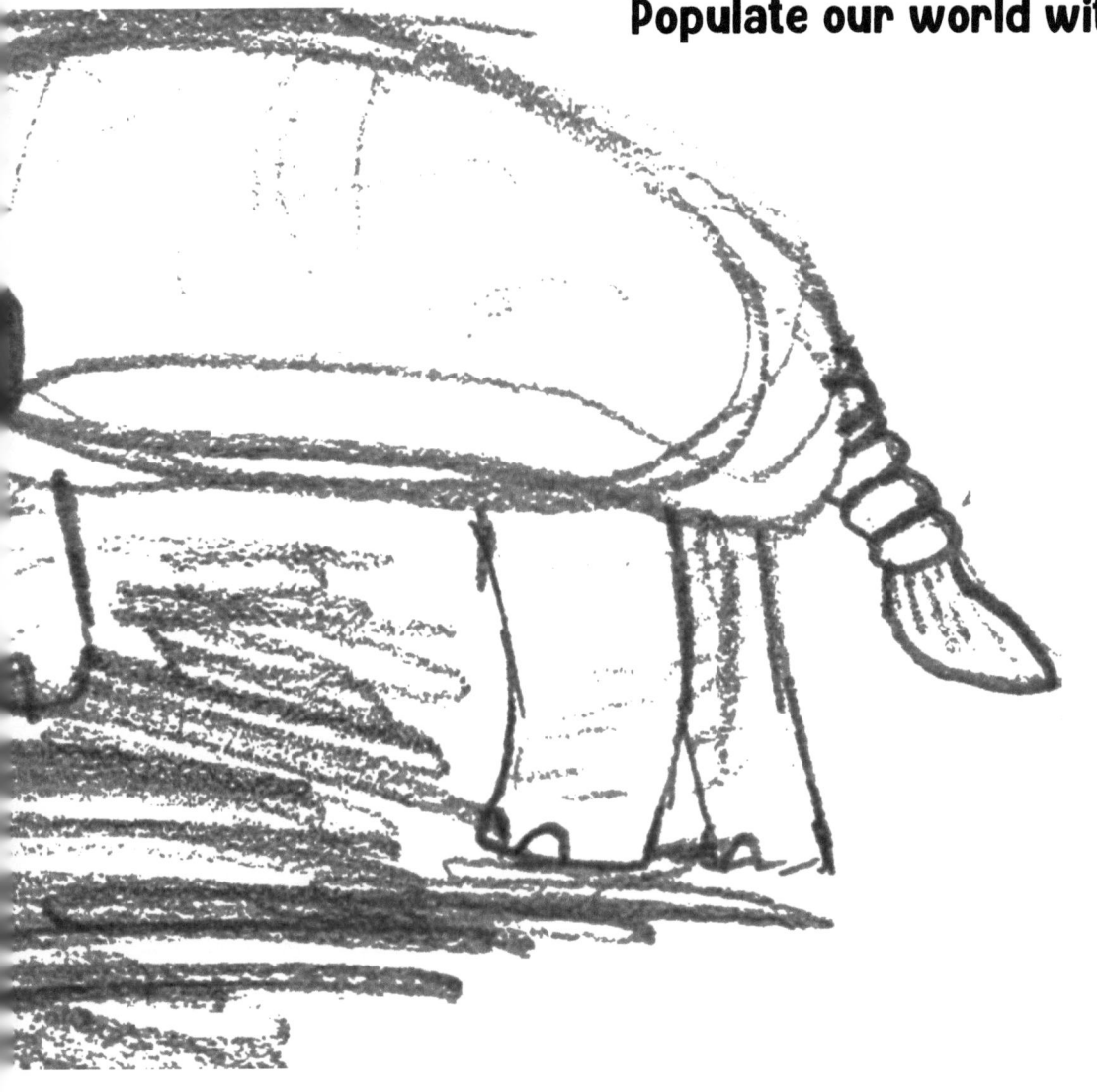

11. Flying Dragon

Behold the flying dragon
A fire breather of sorts
Lightening the horizon
With a few rapid snorts

The dragon is a reminder
Of all the magic in the world
Empowering love and friendship
On a brave knight's crest unfurled

12. Gray Smiling Fog

Life is like living
Within a gray fog
Its smile protects us
From the smelly bog

The fog is part of life
It constantly ebbs and flows
It is something we accept
And acknowledge, I suppose

13. Fireworks

Other times life explodes
Like fireworks in the sky
Bursting illuminations
Celebrations soaring high

Life can be fireworks
Sometimes very steady
Other times erratic
You'd better be ready

14. Sun Fireworks with Aurora

The muddy gray skies above
Reveal the sun's aurora
Lighting the phenomena
To which we are explorers

Even if you feel alone
And think there is no hope
Believe in your anchors
If not, you are a dope

Rating Dexter's Drawings:
Become and art critic and use the spreadsheet below to rate each of Dexter's drawings on a scale of 1 to 10 with 1 being the most fartsy and 10 being the most artsy. Feel free to duplicate the spreadsheet as needed.

ARTS OR FARTS?	Critic 1 Rate 1-10	Critic 2 Rate 1-10	Critic 3 Rate 1-10
1. Self-Portrait			
2. Multiple Eyes			
3. Two Hands			
4. Snail on a Stool			
5. Pyramid Giving Birth			
6. World Buildings			
7. Half Face of Boy with Dog			
8. Two Bananas			
9. Soda Can			
10. Elephant			
11. Flying Dragon			
12 Grey Smiling Fog			
13. Fireworks			
14. Aurora			
Add Up Total			
Divide By 14	÷14	÷14	÷14
FINAL SCORE			

Understand the Tally

You have studied Dexter's art.
and what he can create, so
what will his pictures reveal
about the art or fart debate?

Fill in the numbers
Complete your tally
State your opinion
Don't dilly-dally

Add up all your ratings
then divide by fourteen

The answer to this problem
May range from kind to mean

If your score was 1 to 3
A cutting critic are thee

If your score was 4 to 6
"Mezza-Mezza" are your picks

If you scored 7 to 10
Mastered you the art of zen!

Examine Critical Judgments

Wearing your critic's hat
can the art be worthless?
Condemning the artist
to the state of mirthless

If so remove your critic's hat
Which promotes the insanity
Consider how art may reveal
A more centered humanity

Stifling a person's talent
May seem to some as funny
But darkening our vision
Means lives cannot be sunny

Each one of us
has creativity within
and to discourage it
is nowhere to begin

Everyone needs to grow
without a bully's wrath
As we find our footing
to fulfill our life's path.

When we become intolerant
and know we have all the answers
We are simply wooden puppets
and not vibrant fluid dancers

Mockery of others
Dividing ins from outs
Hurtful, unkind labels
Create most vile pouts

Discrimination will follow
The powerful over the poor
Lashing ugly stereotypes
To keep people insecure

When criticizing others
Always to be judicious
Kindness over cruelty
is simply so delicious

The real challenge moving forward
Is for you to understand
Treating people with dignity
Needs to be spread across the land

We need to recognize
divisiveness and hate
Effectively muzzle
the things which doom our fate

Caste projects expectations
Of how people should behave
Sending human potential
to a frosty early grave

Absolute rights, absolute wrongs
Bullies insist you sing their song
They won't accept a voice off-key
They'll never grasp your rhapsody.

If you assessed the art
without nasty critique
it signals your virtue
of which I now will speak

Humans need community
To help us grow and thrive
Artist provide connections
Connections keep us alive.

Beware of social media
The tycoons need your attention
To market all your privacy
To feed their on-line invention

These gurus promise links
False flag situations
Designed to waste time from
Personal relations

They promise a better way
To communicate your life
But allow hurtful garbage
To create personal strife

Platforms can be humane
Or destroy self-image
An isolate in the cloud
To game you in the scrimmage

May your judgements be honest
Constructive and discerning
Securing conversation
To what we should be learning

Art connects us from A to Z
Showing us what we did not see
If you do not know how to look
You'd better slowly re-read this book

If you understand ideas
Poles and poles and poles apart
Reach beyond their barriers
Break walls and create your art!

Dexter's Drawings: A Guided Discussion

On its surface, this book raises issues about judging art. Underneath it is a vehicle to analyze how making judgements may lead to bullying, intolerance, discrimination, violence, stereotypes, caste expectations and socialmedia isolation/exploitation. It also advocates resolving conflicts by communication, connections, creativity and self-exploration. Giving children the gift to become successful in life means allowing them the time to explore the affective as well as the cognitive sides of learning.

(The following guided discussion is designed for teachers, counselors, school administrators and of course parents, to help children from the 6th grade to high school understand the messages in the book. For lower grades one may need to create a definition list for words readers

may not understand. Pick and choose from the guided questions and suggested strategies you feel would be most helpful promoting a thoughtful discussion)

The Challenge

1. What is Dexter challenging the reader to do? Why do you think he is issuing it?

Judge the Images

1. **Dexter's Self-Portrait:** Should Dexter be concerned about what other people think about his drawings?
2. **Multiple Eyes:** What do you think the eyes symbolize?
3. **Two Hands:** What could your hands do to make the world a better place?
4. **Snail on a Stool:** What do you think the snail's primary motivation was for climbing the stool; to see things better or to show other snails he could rise above them?
5. **Pyramids:** Since it is impossible for inanimate objects to give birth, why did Dexter see pyramids doing so?
6. **World Buildings:** Do cities have a clear purpose for their inhabitants or are they just urban sprawl? Explain.
7. **Half Face of a Boy with a Dog:** To what extent are good friendships important in life? Examples. How do you know when a friendship is good?
8. **Two Bananas and an Apple:** Do people always have clarity in their lives? Give examples to support your position.
9. **Still Life with a Soda Can:** Write down three things you find sweet in life. Circle your top choice. Explain why you feel that choice is the sweetest.
10. **Elephant:** Here Dexter is calling out people who use guns to destroy lives. Based on your experience do you feel he is correct to do so? Explain.
11. **Flying Dragon:** Who does the author want "the brave knight" to be?
12. **Gray Smiling Fog:** Do you think the gray smiling fog could exist if there was no smelly bog? Why or why not?
13. **Fireworks:** When does your life appear steady and when's it erratic? Give an example.
14. **Aurora:** What are the anchors in your life? Why does Dexter feel you need to believe in them?

Understand the Tally

After the spreadsheet rating Dexter's art is completed, have each participant identify him or herself as a cutting critic, mezza-mezza or zen master. Which of the three rating groups best analyzed Dexter's drawings? Why?

Examine Critical Judgments

Divide readers into small groups and assign an appropriate number of versus depending on the number of small groups created. For the verses each group is assigned have them come to written consensus by answering the two questions below:

1. Explain the message behind the images/verses your group was assigned.

2. Can your group share a story which would support of refute that message?

In large group:

1. Select each group to report their findings to the large groups.

2. By a show of hands, if you could go back and change your initial ratings on the spreadsheet, how many of you would do so? What made you change your rating?

3. If you could offer Dexter some advice about his art, what would it be?

4. What advice do you think Dexter would offer some people in this group if he heard their reactions?

www.ingramcontent.com/pod-product-compliance
Lightning Source LLC
Chambersburg PA
CBHW041508220426
43661CB00017B/1282